MUCH ADO

This much loved comedy of William Shakespeare's first appeared in print in 1600. It is about two very different love stories. When the handsome Claudio returns from war, he immediately falls in love with the beautiful Hero, and everybody is happy when they decide to marry. Everybody, that is, except one man, who does his best to break the young couple's hearts.

Love, like war, is not easy. It can be very sad, when things go wrong. But it can also be very funny, for family and friends who enjoy watching the young lovers. Benedick and Beatrice are not a sweet, loving couple like Claudio and Hero. They both hate the idea of marriage. 'I shall never be a husband,' says Benedick. And if Beatrice is asked when she will marry, she answers, 'Never, I hope.' But their friends have a secret plan . . .

William Shakespeare (1564–1616) was an actor, poet and playwright, who lived and worked in Stratford-upon-Avon and London. He wrote more than thirty plays, which are still discussed and performed all over the world today. He is generally considered the greatest writer in the English language.

OXFORD BOOKWORMS PLAYSCRIPTS

Series Editor: Clare West

OXFORD BOOKWORMS

For a full list of titles in all the Oxford Bookworms series,
please refer to the *Oxford English* catalogue.

OXFORD BOOKWORMS PLAYSCRIPTS

Stage 1
The Murder of Mary Jones *Tim Vicary*

A Ghost in Love and Other Plays *Michael Dean*

Sherlock Holmes: Two Plays
Sir Arthur Conan Doyle (retold by John Escott)

Stage 2
The Importance of Being Earnest
Oscar Wilde (retold by Susan Kingsley)

Much Ado About Nothing
William Shakespeare (retold by Alistair McCallum)

Romeo & Juliet
William Shakespeare (retold by Alistair McCallum)

WILLIAM SHAKESPEARE

Much Ado About Nothing

Retold by
Alistair McCallum

OXFORD UNIVERSITY PRESS
2000

Oxford University Press,
Great Clarendon Street, Oxford OX2 6DP

Oxford New York

Athens Auckland Bangkok Bogotá Buenos Aires Calcutta Cape Town
Chennai Dar es Salaam Delhi Florence Hong Kong Istanbul Karachi
Kuala Lumpur Madrid Melbourne Mexico City Mumbai Nairobi
Paris São Paulo Singapore Taipei Tokyo Toronto Warsaw
and associated companies in
Berlin Ibadan

OXFORD and OXFORD ENGLISH
are trade marks of Oxford University Press
ISBN 0 19 422857 6

Printed in Hong Kong

INTRODUCTION

Much Ado About Nothing is set in Messina, a town on the Mediterranean island of Sicily, about four hundred years ago. Sicily is Italian now, but in Shakespeare's time it had Spanish rulers. When the play begins, the Spanish prince, Don Pedro, and his Italian gentlemen are coming to Messina after fighting in a war. They are going to stay for some time at the house of Leonato, Lord of Messina.

PERFORMANCE NOTES

Act 1   Scene 1: Leonato's garden, outside his house
        Scene 2: A room in Leonato's house
Act 2   Scene 1: A large room in Leonato's house
        Scene 2: A smaller room in Leonato's house
        Scene 3: Leonato's garden
Act 3   Scene 1: Leonato's garden
        Scene 2: A room in Leonato's house
        Scene 3: A street in Messina, with a low wall
Act 4   Scene 1: Outside a church
        Scene 2: In the Messina prison
Act 5   Scene 1: A street in Messina
        Scene 2: Leonato's garden
        Scene 3: A room in Leonato's house

You will need a rolled-up letter, tables and chairs, glasses and bottles, some paper for Verges to write on, masks, and musical instruments. In Leonato's garden there must be a tree to hide behind.

～

CHARACTERS IN THE PLAY

Leonato, Lord of Messina

Hero, Leonato's daughter

Beatrice, Hero's cousin

Margaret and **Ursula,** Hero's servants

Don Pedro, Prince of Aragon

Benedick, a young gentleman, and friend of Don Pedro's

Claudio, a young gentleman, and friend of Don Pedro's

Don John, Don Pedro's brother

Borachio and **Conrade,** Don John's servants

Father Francis, a priest

Dogberry, the head of the police

Verges, a policeman

Three other policemen

Musicians

Two messengers

Much Ado About Nothing

The soldiers come back from the war

Outside Leonato's house, in Messina. Leonato is talking to Hero and Beatrice. A messenger arrives with a letter.

MESSENGER My lord Leonato, this letter is for you.

LEONATO Thank you. (*He reads the letter.*)

HERO What does it say, father? Is it about the war?

LEONATO Yes, my dear. It's from my friend Don Pedro. It says that the war has finished.

HERO That's wonderful news!

LEONATO It says that the soldiers are coming back to Messina today. Don Pedro is coming to see us.

HERO Are many of the soldiers hurt?

MESSENGER No, my lady, only a few.

LEONATO This letter says that Claudio, a young gentleman from Florence, was very brave.

BEATRICE What about the Lion of Messina, the bravest man in the world? (*She laughs.*)

LEONATO I don't understand. Who are you talking about, Beatrice?

HERO She means Benedick, father, a friend of Don Pedro's.

'Welcome to Messina!'

BEATRICE That's right. He thinks that he's the bravest
man in the world, but he isn't. He doesn't like
fighting. He prefers watching other people fight.

MESSENGER That's not true! Benedick is a good soldier.

HERO Don't be angry. My cousin Beatrice likes
Benedick, but she laughs at him all the time.

LEONATO Here they come! (*Don Pedro, Don John,
Claudio and Benedick enter.*) Don Pedro!
Welcome to Messina!

DON PEDRO Leonato! It's good to see you again. You
already know my friend Benedick, don't you?

BEATRICE Of course he does. Benedick is the most
famous man in the world. Everyone knows him.

DON PEDRO And this is Claudio.

2

LEONATO Welcome, gentlemen. This is my daughter,
Hero, and her cousin, Beatrice.

BENEDICK Ah, Beatrice – we've already met, haven't we?

BEATRICE Have we? I can't remember. (*All laugh.*)

BENEDICK You never remember anything, Beatrice –
you're always too busy talking.

BEATRICE Perhaps my words are more interesting than
yours, Benedick. (*She turns away from him.*)

DON PEDRO Leonato, this is my brother, Don John. He
was my enemy for many years, but now we are
friends again.

LEONATO That's good. Don Pedro, I hope with all my
heart that you, your brother and your friends
will stay here at my house for some time. Would
you like to come inside?

'Perhaps my words are more interesting than yours, Benedick.'

Everyone leaves except Claudio and Benedick.

CLAUDIO Benedick, did you see Leonato's daughter?

BENEDICK Yes, of course I did. Why? Do you like her?

CLAUDIO Like her? I love her!

BENEDICK What? You've only met her once! She's very
sweet, but . . .

CLAUDIO Sweet? She's the most beautiful girl I've ever
seen! Benedick, I'm going to marry her if I can!

Don Pedro enters.

DON PEDRO Come on, you two! Come inside!

BENEDICK Claudio has some interesting news, Don
Pedro. He's in love.

DON PEDRO Really?

CLAUDIO I love Hero. I want to marry her.

DON PEDRO That's wonderful! I think the two of you will
be very happy if you marry.

BENEDICK Ha! It's impossible for anyone to be married
and to be happy. I tell you, *I* shall never be a
husband!

DON PEDRO Oh yes, you will! One day soon, Claudio and
I will call you 'Benedick, the married man'.
Now, go into the house and tell Leonato that
we'll be with him soon.

*Benedick leaves. Borachio enters. He hides, and the
others don't see him. He listens carefully.*

CLAUDIO Don Pedro, you must help me. I love Hero, but

'I tell you, I shall never be a husband!'

I don't know if she loves me. I want to marry
her, but perhaps her father won't agree. What
can I do?

DON PEDRO Don't worry. Leonato is an old friend of
mine. I'll talk to him.

CLAUDIO But what about Hero? I don't know what to
say to her. She's so beautiful!

DON PEDRO Listen, there'll be a party here tonight. I'll tell
Hero that you love her. I'll ask her if she wants
to marry you. She'll say yes, I'm sure.

CLAUDIO Oh, I hope so! Thank you, my lord.

Claudio and Don Pedro leave.

BORACHIO So Claudio wants to marry Leonato's
daughter. My master, Don John, will find that
very interesting!

ACT 1 SCENE 2
Don John hears a secret

A room in Leonato's house. Don John and his servant Conrade are talking.

CONRADE What's the matter, my lord? You look unhappy.

DON JOHN I look unhappy because I *am* unhappy.

CONRADE But why, Don John? You and your brother Don Pedro are friends now.

DON JOHN Don't talk to me about my brother! I hate him. He thinks that we are friends, but I'm still angry with him. I'm angry with all of them – Leonato, Claudio . . .

CONRADE But why?

DON JOHN Stop asking so many questions, Conrade! My brother is my enemy, and so are all his friends. Do you understand?

CONRADE Yes, my lord. But you must try to *look* happy if you want your brother to think that you don't hate him any more.

DON JOHN You are right, Conrade. I hate them all, but I will smile lovingly at them. Here comes Borachio – and he's in a hurry!

Borachio runs into the room.

BORACHIO Don John, I have some news. Claudio wants to marry Leonato's daughter!

DON JOHN How do you know?

BORACHIO I heard your brother and Claudio talking a few minutes ago. Claudio wants to marry Hero, and Don Pedro is going to help him. It's a secret!

CONRADE Didn't they see you?

BORACHIO No. I was hiding. They didn't know that I was listening.

DON JOHN That brave young gentleman Claudio, and the beautiful Hero! How I hate them! But I can make trouble for them. Will you both help me?

CONRADE To the death, my lord!

DON JOHN Come, let us talk about our plans.

BORACHIO We will follow you, my lord. (*They leave.*)

Conrade, Don John and Borachio.

ACT 2 SCENE 1
Don John tries to make trouble

Inside Leonato's house. Leonato, Hero, Beatrice, their servants Ursula and Margaret, and the musicians are all getting ready for the party.

LEONATO Now, are you all ready? Our guests will be here in a few minutes. Ursula, Margaret – bring in the food. Hero, my dear, you look beautiful.

BEATRICE Perhaps she'll fall in love tonight!

LEONATO What about you, Beatrice? When will you marry?

BEATRICE Never, I hope.

HERO But why not? Don't you like men?

BEATRICE Of course I do. My father was a man, and I liked him. My brother is a man, and I like him.

HERO (*Smiling*) Benedick is a man.

BEATRICE And I hate him! He talks too much, he laughs too much, and . . .

LEONATO Here they come! Welcome, gentlemen!

Don Pedro, Claudio and Benedick enter, wearing masks.

LEONATO Musicians – start playing! Listen, everyone! I want you all to dance and enjoy yourselves. (*The musicians play, and some people start dancing.*)

DON PEDRO (*To Hero*) Would you like to dance with me?

HERO   Perhaps. Who are you?

DON PEDRO   I won't tell you my name. Come and sit down first! (*They go to the side of the room and talk.*)

BENEDICK   (*To Beatrice*) Are you Beatrice?

BEATRICE   Yes, that's right. Why, who are you?

BENEDICK   I won't tell you! Someone was talking about you last week. He said, 'Beatrice is an angry old woman. Don't go near her – she's always arguing!' I can't remember who it was.

BEATRICE   I know – it was that idiot Benedick!

BENEDICK   Oh! Er – who's Benedick?

BEATRICE   Don't you know him? He's the most boring man I've ever known. He thinks that all the women in Messina are in love with him. But everyone just laughs at him!

'I know – it was that idiot Benedick!'

9

BENEDICK Oh. When I meet him, I'll tell him what you say.

Benedick, Beatrice and Leonato go to the side of the
room. Don John, Borachio and Conrade enter.

DON JOHN Borachio – is that Claudio over there, wearing
his mask?

BORACHIO Yes, my lord. I know the way he stands.

DON JOHN Now for my plan. (*To Claudio*) You're
Benedick, aren't you? Listen, Benedick. My
brother Don Pedro is in love with Hero.

BORACHIO That's right, sir, he's going to marry her.

CLAUDIO What! Is this true? How do you know?

CONRADE I heard them talking a few minutes ago. Look
– they're together now. Can't you see?

DON JOHN My brother is making a mistake, isn't he,
Benedick? He is a prince, and he must marry a
king's daughter. Hero is not good enough for
him. Why don't you talk to him, Benedick? He
will listen to you.

Don John, Borachio and Conrade leave. Benedick
comes to talk to Claudio.

BENEDICK Is that you, Claudio?

CLAUDIO Yes, it's me. Let's take off our masks. (*They*
take them off.) I've just heard some terrible news,
Benedick. Don Pedro is going to marry Hero!

BENEDICK What! But *you* love Hero, don't you?

CLAUDIO I thought that Don Pedro was my friend, and

10

'What's the matter with Claudio?'

wanted to help me. Oh Hero, my lost love!

Claudio leaves, and Don Pedro comes to find Benedick.

DON PEDRO Ah, Benedick. Where's Claudio gone? Why is
he in such a hurry? What's the matter?

BENEDICK He's angry with you, Don Pedro. Why did you
steal Hero from him?

DON PEDRO But I didn't! I told Hero that Claudio loves
her. She's very happy, and wants to marry him.
I've talked to her father, and he agrees.

BENEDICK I don't understand. Claudio heard that . . .

DON PEDRO Here comes Claudio now, with Beatrice.

Beatrice and Claudio come over to them.

BENEDICK Oh, no! My lord, I will do anything you ask. I
will go to the end of the world, fight a hundred
men or kill a lion, but do not ask me to spend
another minute with that woman! (*He leaves.*)

11

DON PEDRO   Claudio, I have some wonderful news.

CLAUDIO   I know. It's about Hero.

DON PEDRO   Aren't you happy? Hero wants to marry you!

CLAUDIO   Marry *me*? But – isn't she going to marry *you*?

DON PEDRO   Of course not! Here comes Leonato now.

Leonato and Hero come to talk to them.

LEONATO   Claudio, Don Pedro has spoken to me, and I
          know that you love my daughter. Take her as
          your wife, and be happy!

BEATRICE   Say something, Claudio!

Hero and Claudio.

CLAUDIO I . . . I can't find the right words. (*To Hero*)
Lady, if you are mine, then I am yours.

BEATRICE (*To Hero*) Speak, cousin, or close his mouth
with a kiss. (*Claudio and Hero kiss.*)

DON PEDRO What about you, Beatrice? Where shall we
find a husband for you?

BEATRICE Don't talk to me about husbands, my lord! It's
late. I'm going to bed. (*She leaves.*)

DON PEDRO (*To Leonato*) I have an idea. I think that the
best husband for Beatrice would be Benedick.

LEONATO What! That's impossible! They argue every
time they meet.

CLAUDIO Benedick says that he'll never marry.

HERO And Beatrice says that *she'll* never marry!

DON PEDRO Listen. I have a plan. If the three of you agree
to help me, I think that there'll soon be another
wedding in Messina.

ACT 2 SCENE 2
Borachio has an idea

*A room in Leonato's house. Don John, Conrade and
Borachio are talking.*

DON JOHN What happened at the party, Conrade? Is
Claudio angry with Don Pedro? Did they fight?

13

CONRADE No, my lord. They all talked together, and Claudio and Hero are going to marry soon.

DON JOHN No! We must stop them! Claudio is my brother's friend. I don't want him to be happy. I hate them all!

BORACHIO I have an idea, Don John. Hero has a servant called Margaret. She is a friend of mine.

DON JOHN Go on, Borachio.

BORACHIO On the night before Hero's wedding, I'll tell Margaret to wear Hero's clothes. I'll tell her to go into Hero's bedroom – when Hero isn't there – and to open the window.

CONRADE So if people see her, they'll think that she is Hero. But why?

BORACHIO Listen. I will be in Hero's room too. When Margaret opens the window, I'll call out loudly, 'Hero, my love, close the window and come back to me.'

DON JOHN If Claudio sees this, he'll be very angry! He'll never speak to Hero again.

BORACHIO My lord, you must tell Claudio and Don Pedro to come and watch while I speak to Margaret.

CONRADE They'll think that Hero has a lover. There'll be trouble!

DON JOHN Borachio, if this plan works, I'll pay you well – in gold!

Act 2 Scene 3

A surprise for Benedick

Benedick is alone in Leonato's garden.

BENEDICK Why do people marry? Claudio is a brave
      soldier, and a wonderful fighter, but now he only
      talks about love. Will that ever happen to me?
      No! I like women, but I'm never going to marry.

Don Pedro, Leonato and Claudio enter.

BENEDICK I don't want to talk to them. If I hide behind
      this tree, they won't see me. (*He hides.*)

DON PEDRO (*Quietly, to Leonato and Claudio*) Now, you
      two, remember our plan. Benedick's hiding behind
      the tree. Speak loudly, and then he'll hear us.

'Remember our plan!'

15

LEONATO (*Loudly*) Don Pedro, my daughter told me a
secret this morning.

DON PEDRO What did she say, Leonato?

LEONATO That Beatrice is in love.

BENEDICK (*To himself*) What!

CLAUDIO That's right, Don Pedro. Hero told me too.
Beatrice is in love – with Benedick.

BENEDICK (*To himself*) With me? I don't believe it!

DON PEDRO But Beatrice is always laughing at Benedick.
She says that she'll never fall in love with any man!

LEONATO She loves him, but she doesn't want to tell him.

CLAUDIO Leonato is right, Don Pedro. Once she wrote a
love letter to Benedick, but she didn't send it.

DON PEDRO So Beatrice loves Benedick. What a surprise!
But if she doesn't tell him, he will never know.

CLAUDIO And if she tells him, he'll laugh at her. What
can she do? She's very unhappy.

LEONATO She's a beautiful girl.

CLAUDIO And she's kind.

DON PEDRO And she's clever.

CLAUDIO So why does she love Benedick? (*They laugh.*)

BENEDICK (*To himself*) What! Why are they laughing?

*Leonato, Claudio and Don Pedro leave. Benedick comes
out from behind the tree.*

BENEDICK I can't believe it! Beatrice loves me! That's what
Leonato said – it must be true! They all think that

16

she is beautiful, and clever. Perhaps they are
right . . . but why does she always laugh at me?

Beatrice enters.

BEATRICE Dinner is ready. Are you coming in?

BENEDICK Ah, Beatrice! I've heard a little secret.

BEATRICE What are you talking about? Oh, it doesn't
matter. I'm hungry, so I'm going inside. If you
want dinner, come in now. (*She leaves.*)

BENEDICK Oh, Beatrice! She loves me – that's why she
came here to find me. The others were right. She
is beautiful, and kind too. Oh, how I love her!
Beatrice – wait for me! I'll come with you!

ACT 3 SCENE 1
A surprise for Beatrice

Hero, Margaret and Ursula are in Leonato's garden.

HERO Margaret, go and find Beatrice. Tell her to come
out into the garden.

MARGARET What shall I say to her?

HERO Tell her that Ursula and I are talking about her.

URSULA That's right, tell her that she must come and
listen secretly. (*Margaret leaves.*)

HERO Now, remember the plan, Ursula. We must talk
about Benedick, and how much he loves Beatrice.

'Remember, Ursula – speak loudly!'

URSULA   Sh! Here she comes now. (*Beatrice enters.*)

BEATRICE   (*To herself*) Margaret says that Hero and Ursula are talking about me. How strange! I'll hide behind this tree and listen. (*She hides.*)

HERO   (*To Ursula*) Remember, Ursula – speak loudly!

URSULA   (*Loudly*) So Benedick's in love, is he?

HERO   That's right. His friends told me. He's in love with Beatrice.

BEATRICE   (*To herself*) What! Benedick – in love with me?

URSULA   Shall we tell Beatrice?

HERO   No, Ursula, we mustn't tell her. If she hears that Benedick loves her, she'll only laugh at him.

BEATRICE   (*To herself*) What! No, I won't!

URSULA   Poor Benedick! He's in love, but he can't say anything to Beatrice.

HERO   No. He's very unhappy.

URSULA If he's lucky, perhaps he will meet someone
kinder than Beatrice.

HERO I hope so. He's a good man. He's very brave.

URSULA And he's very good-looking. I think he's the best
man in Italy.

HERO No, Ursula, Claudio is the best man in Italy.
That's why I'm going to marry him!

URSULA They are both fine men. Come, my lady, let's go
inside.

Hero and Ursula leave. Beatrice comes out.

BEATRICE Can this really be true? Does Benedick love
me? Everyone thinks that I hate him, but it's not
true. Hero and Ursula are right – he is brave, and
good-looking. Oh, Benedick! I love you!

ACT 3 SCENE 2
Claudio hears a terrible secret

*A room in Leonato's house. Leonato, Don Pedro,
Claudio and Benedick are talking.*

DON PEDRO Leonato, I have enjoyed staying with you.
But tomorrow, after Claudio's wedding, I must
go home.

LEONATO Stay as long as you want, Don Pedro. You
must stay too, Benedick.

BENEDICK Sorry? I wasn't listening, my lord.

DON PEDRO What's the matter, Benedick? What are you thinking about?

BENEDICK Nothing, my lord.

CLAUDIO Perhaps he's in love.

BENEDICK Of course not! I – er – I've got toothache.

DON PEDRO Toothache! I don't believe you, Benedick. I agree with Claudio. I think you're in love.

CLAUDIO I think I know someone who is dying of love for Benedick. (*Claudio and Don Pedro laugh.*)

BENEDICK I'm not listening, Claudio! My lord Leonato, can I talk to you? (*Benedick and Leonato leave.*)

DON PEDRO They're going to talk about Beatrice!

CLAUDIO Your plan has gone well, Don Pedro. (*Don John enters.*) Look – here's your brother.

DON PEDRO It's good to see you, brother John. How are you?

DON JOHN I have some bad news, my friends. Claudio, are you planning to marry tomorrow?

CLAUDIO Yes, I am. Everyone knows that I am going to marry Leonato's daughter, Hero.

DON JOHN I'm sorry, but I must tell you something that will hurt you – the truth about Hero.

DON PEDRO What are you talking about?

DON JOHN She has a secret life. She doesn't love you.

CLAUDIO That's a terrible thing to say!

DON JOHN   Perhaps she says that she loves you. But she has many, many lovers. You are not the only one.

DON PEDRO   My brother, how can you say that? Hero is a sweet young girl. She wants to marry Claudio. She doesn't love any other man.

DON JOHN   I know that this is bad news for you. But if you come with me tonight, you'll understand.

CLAUDIO   What do you mean? What will we see?

DON JOHN   One of Hero's lovers is going to visit her at midnight tonight.

DON PEDRO   What! The night before her wedding?

DON JOHN   Come with me to Hero's window tonight, and you will see that I am right.

CLAUDIO   This is terrible. If this is true, I will never marry Hero. (*Claudio and Don Pedro leave.*)

DON JOHN   Borachio! (*Borachio enters.*) You remember the plan, don't you?

BORACHIO   Yes, my lord. I'll be in Hero's bedroom at midnight tonight.

'Hero is a sweet young girl.'

21

'I'll be in Hero's bedroom at midnight tonight.'

DON JOHN   And will Margaret be there?

BORACHIO   Yes, my lord. She'll wear Hero's clothes, and she'll open the window.

DON JOHN   Good. Remember that Claudio and Don Pedro will be in the garden, watching.

BORACHIO   When Margaret goes to the window, I'll call out to her and tell her that I love her.

DON JOHN   Good. There will be trouble, Borachio! Claudio is going to be very unhappy – and so is Hero!

ACT 3 SCENE 3
The police find two criminals

A street, late at night. Dogberry is talking to Verges and three other policemen.

DOGBERRY   Now, you know what your job is, don't you?

1ST POLICEMAN   Yes, sir, we're policemen.

22

DOGBERRY I know that you're policemen! I mean, do you know what you must do?

2ND POLICEMAN Yes, sir. We must walk around Messina. If we see any trouble, we must stop it.

VERGES That's right. If you meet any thieves, tell them to stop stealing at once.

3RD POLICEMAN What if they don't stop, sir?

DOGBERRY Well, tell them to leave Messina and steal from another town.

2ND POLICEMAN And if we find anyone shouting or making too much noise, we'll tell them to be quiet.

VERGES That's right. We don't want any trouble.

1ST POLICEMAN And we'll go to all the public houses.

VERGES That's a good idea. Walking around Messina all night is very boring. It's cold, too.

DOGBERRY No, Verges, he means that they'll go to the public houses to see if there's any trouble.

3RD POLICEMAN That's right, sir. If we find any people who have drunk too much, we'll tell them to go home.

DOGBERRY That's right, men. Now, Verges, come with me. (*Dogberry and Verges leave.*)

1ST POLICEMAN Let's see if we can find any criminals.

2ND POLICEMAN Wait a minute! I can hear voices.

3RD POLICEMAN Let's hide behind this wall.

They hide. Borachio and Conrade enter.

CONRADE A hundred pounds? In gold?

BORACHIO   That's right, Don John's given me a hundred
     pounds. I've just been to Hero's room.

CONRADE   Was Margaret there?

BORACHIO   Yes, and she was wearing Hero's clothes. I
     shouted, 'Hero, my love, give me a kiss!'

He laughs.

CONRADE   Were Claudio and Don Pedro watching?

BORACHIO   Yes, they were in the garden with Don John.

CONRADE   Claudio won't marry Hero now, will he?

BORACHIO   Never! That's why Don John has given me a
     hundred pounds. He's very happy – and so am I!
     Here – let's have a drink!

*He takes a bottle from his pocket. The policemen jump
out and take hold of the two men.*

1ST POLICEMAN   Stop, both of you! Stay where you are, in
     the Prince's name!

CONRADE   Take your hands off us! We haven't done
     anything wrong.

2ND POLICEMAN   Oh yes, you have! We heard everything.
     You have said terrible things about Lady Hero.

3RD POLICEMAN   And they're thieves. This man has stolen
     a hundred pounds.

BORACHIO   No, I haven't! It's my money!

2ND POLICEMAN   Let's take them to the prison. Dogberry
     will want to ask them some questions.

3RD POLICEMAN   Come on, you two! Come with us!

ACT 4 SCENE 1

Hero's wedding day

Outside the church. Father Francis, Leonato, Hero, Beatrice and Benedick are ready for the wedding.

LEONATO Hero, my dear, this is a very happy day for me.

HERO And for me too, father.

Don Pedro, Claudio and Don John enter.

LEONATO Here comes Claudio! Father Francis, the wedding can begin now.

FATHER FRANCIS Claudio and Hero, you have come here today to marry. Hero, do you agree to be Claudio's wife?

HERO I do.

FATHER FRANCIS And Claudio, do you agree to be Hero's husband?

CLAUDIO No! (*Everyone shouts in surprise.*)

LEONATO What! Claudio, you mustn't joke like this.

HERO My love, what's the matter?

CLAUDIO You heard what I said. Leonato, I will not marry your daughter.

LEONATO This is terrible! What's happened, Claudio?

CLAUDIO Everyone thinks that Hero is a good, sweet young girl. It's not true. She has many lovers.

BEATRICE How can you say that about my cousin?

'How can you say that about my cousin?'

LEONATO I don't believe you, Claudio! Don Pedro, why
    is he saying these things?

DON PEDRO I'm sorry, Leonato, but Claudio is right.

HERO No! Listen to me, all of you! Claudio is the only
    man that I love!

DON PEDRO A man was in Hero's room last night. We
    heard them laughing, and we saw them kissing at
    the window.

DON JOHN It's true, Leonato. One of Hero's lovers visited
    her last night. It has happened many times.

HERO I talked with no man last night, my lord.

Claudio, Don Pedro and Don John leave. Hero faints.

BEATRICE (*Holding Hero*) Hero! My dear cousin!

BENEDICK How is she? She's not dead, is she?

FATHER FRANCIS No, she's alive. She's opening her eyes.

LEONATO   This is the worst day of my life. What are we going to do?

BENEDICK   Sir, I just do not know what to say.

BEATRICE   I'm sure that Hero hasn't done anything wrong.

FATHER FRANCIS   I agree with you. Hero, did anyone visit you last night?

HERO   No, of course not. Kill me if you like, but please don't believe Claudio and Don Pedro!

FATHER FRANCIS   Listen. I have a plan. We'll tell Don Pedro, Claudio and all the others that Hero is dead.

LEONATO   Dead? Why, Father?

FATHER FRANCIS   If they think that Hero is dead, they will not be angry with her any more. Then, perhaps, they will be able to find out the truth.

LEONATO   Very well, Father, I agree. We will tell everyone that Hero is dead.

Everyone except Benedick and Beatrice leaves.

BENEDICK   Don't cry, Beatrice.

BEATRICE   This is a terrible day for my cousin Hero.

BENEDICK   Beatrice, there's something that I must tell you. I love you more than anything in the world. And I know that you love me.

BEATRICE   What! How do you know? Who told you?

BENEDICK   That doesn't matter. You love me, don't you?

'I love you with all my heart.'

BEATRICE I don't know what to say. (*They kiss.*) Yes, I love you with all my heart.

BENEDICK Beatrice, I will do anything for you.

BEATRICE Kill Claudio.

BENEDICK What? No, not for the world! Claudio is my friend.

BEATRICE Then you do not really love me! My cousin's heart is broken, and it's all because of your friends, the brave Claudio and the good Don Pedro!

BENEDICK Beatrice, I'm sorry about Hero. But I love *you*, and that's the most important thing.

BEATRICE You love your friends more than me. Go,
Benedick, and leave me alone.

BENEDICK But aren't Don Pedro and Claudio telling the
truth? They said that there was someone in
Hero's room last night.

BEATRICE If they believe that, they are stupid.

BENEDICK I'm sorry, Beatrice. You are right. Claudio has
hurt your cousin badly. I will fight him, and one
of us will die. (*He kisses her hand and leaves.*)

ACT 4 SCENE 2
Dogberry talks to the prisoners

*Borachio and Conrade are in prison. Dogberry and
Verges have come to ask them some questions. The
policemen are watching.*

DOGBERRY Where are the criminals?

VERGES They are here, sir, in front of you.

DOGBERRY What are your names?

BORACHIO My name is Borachio, and this is my friend
Conrade.

DOGBERRY Well, Borachio and Conrade, I have heard that
you have said bad things about a lady. Also, you
are thieves and you drink too much. Is this true?

BORACHIO No, sir. We haven't done anything wrong.

29

CONRADE That's right, sir. We were walking along the
     street last night when the police suddenly stopped
     us. I don't know why they stopped us, sir.

BORACHIO We'd like to go home, please, sir. We don't
     like being in prison.

DOGBERRY Oh. Verges, there has been a mistake. These
     men say that they aren't criminals.

VERGES Why don't we ask the policemen what they
     think, sir?

DOGBERRY That's a good idea, Verges. Well, men, what
     happened last night?

1ST POLICEMAN While these two men were talking, sir, we
     were hiding behind a wall.

2ND POLICEMAN We heard everything that they said, sir.

3RD POLICEMAN One of them said that he was in Lady
     Hero's bedroom with Margaret, her servant.

VERGES In Hero's bedroom? Perhaps they are thieves?

3RD POLICEMAN One of them had a hundred pounds.

DOGBERRY Ah! So they *are* thieves!

BORACHIO That's not true, sir! (*To Conrade*) This man is
     an idiot, Conrade. What can we do?

DOGBERRY What! I heard you! Verges, that man called
     me an idiot. Write it down!

VERGES Yes, sir. (*He writes.*) You are an idiot, sir.

DOGBERRY That's right. I am an idiot, Verges, remember
     that. These two men are criminals, I think.

VERGES   What shall we do with them, sir? Shall we leave
        them in prison, or shall we tell them to go home?
DOGBERRY   We must ask Lord Leonato – he will decide.
        Let's take them to see him now!

ACT 5 SCENE 1
Borachio tells the truth

Don Pedro and Claudio are walking along the street.

DON PEDRO   Claudio, have you heard that Hero is dead?
CLAUDIO   Yes, I have. But perhaps it's better for her to be
        dead than alive.
Leonato enters.
DON PEDRO   Good morning, my lord.
LEONATO   Good? Nothing is good any more. My
        daughter, my only child, is dead.
CLAUDIO   Sir, we are sorry about Hero's death.
LEONATO   How can you say that? You killed her!
CLAUDIO   That's not true! I didn't want her to die!
DON PEDRO   Leonato, you must remember that we saw
        Hero with another man the night before the
        wedding.
LEONATO   Ha! I don't believe you. And I'll find out the
        truth! (*He leaves, and Benedick enters.*)
CLAUDIO   It's good to see you, Benedick.

31

BENEDICK (*Angrily*) Claudio, you and I are friends no
more.

DON PEDRO What do you mean? Are you joking?

BENEDICK No, I'm not joking. Claudio, you have killed a
sweet lady. And I am going to kill you.

CLAUDIO If you want to fight, I'm not afraid.

BENEDICK When you decide on the time and the place,
send a messenger to tell me. We will meet, and
we will fight. And one of us will die.

DON PEDRO Benedick, what are you saying? Claudio
didn't kill Hero.

BENEDICK My lord, do you know that your brother Don
John has left Messina? I must go now too.

He leaves.

CLAUDIO If he wants to fight, I'm ready!

DON PEDRO No, you mustn't fight. I'll talk to Benedick.
So my brother has left Messina. How strange!

Dogberry, Verges, the policemen and the prisoners enter.

CLAUDIO Look! There are your brother's servants.

DON PEDRO What's the matter, Dogberry? What have
these men done?

DOGBERRY They have done many things, sir. First, they
are criminals. Third, they are thieves.

VERGES And sixth, they drink too much. Second, and
last, they have said bad things about a lady, Lord
Leonato's daughter.

'What have these men done?'

DOGBERRY And fourth, this man said that I was an idiot.
　　　Verges, go and find Lord Leonato and bring him
　　　here. (*Verges leaves.*)

CLAUDIO (*Laughing*) These men are too clever for me,
　　　Don Pedro. I don't understand them.

DON PEDRO Neither do I. What's happened, Borachio?

BORACHIO My lords, do you remember seeing Hero and
　　　her lover the night before the wedding?

CLAUDIO Of course we do!

BORACHIO The woman wasn't Hero, sir. It was her
　　　servant Margaret. And the man wasn't her lover.
　　　It was me.

CLAUDIO What! I don't believe it!

CONRADE It's true, sir. Don John wanted to hurt you and
　　　Hero. He paid Borachio a lot of money to do it.

33

DON PEDRO So Hero didn't do anything wrong.

CLAUDIO Oh, sweet Hero! What have I done? I'm sorry!

DON PEDRO She's dead, Claudio. She'll never come back.

Leonato and Verges enter.

BORACHIO My lord, I'm sorry. I killed your daughter.

LEONATO Not you alone, Borachio. Four men killed my
daughter. You are one of them. Don John is
another. The other two are here now: the brave
Claudio and the good Don Pedro.

CLAUDIO My lord, we are both very sorry. But we
believed Don John when he told us about Hero.

DON PEDRO We made
a terrible
mistake,
Leonato.

LEONATO Claudio,
you killed my
daughter, but
I am not going
to kill you.
My brother
has a daughter.
She is just like
Hero. Will
you marry
her?

'I am very sorry, my lord.'

34

CLAUDIO Of course, my lord! I will do anything you ask.

LEONATO Claudio, Don Pedro, come to my house tomorrow morning. Until then, goodbye.

Act 5 Scene 2
Beatrice and Benedick hear the news

Beatrice and Benedick are in Leonato's garden.

BENEDICK Beatrice, I love you. I think that I have always loved you.

BEATRICE I love you too, Benedick. But do you remember what I asked you to do?

BENEDICK Yes, my love. I have talked to Claudio. I will fight him, and kill him if I can.

BEATRICE Good. My cousin Hero is still very ill.

BENEDICK Beatrice, my love, when did you first fall in love with me? And why?

BEATRICE I didn't want to fall in love with you, or anyone. But when I knew that . . .

Ursula enters, running.

URSULA My lord! My lady! There's some exciting news about Hero! And Don John's servants are in trouble! Come inside and hear about it!

'Beatrice, Hero, Margaret – put on your masks.'

Act 5 Scene 3
Two weddings

Leonato, Father Francis, Beatrice, Hero, Benedick, the servants and musicians are all at Leonato's house.

LEONATO You were right, Father Francis. My daughter didn't do anything wrong.

FATHER FRANCIS Of course she didn't.

LEONATO It was Don John who planned all this. But he has escaped, and nobody knows where he is.

BENEDICK I told Claudio to be ready to fight me, but now I hope that we will be friends.

LEONATO I hope so, too. Claudio will be here soon.

Beatrice, Hero, Margaret – put on your masks.

Don Pedro and Claudio enter.

LEONATO Welcome, gentlemen. Claudio, here is the new wife that I have found for you.

CLAUDIO Can I see her, my lord?

LEONATO First you must agree to marry her.

Hero comes up to Claudio.

FATHER FRANCIS This is the lady. Will you marry her?

CLAUDIO Yes, I will. (*Hero takes off her mask.*) Hero!

DON PEDRO But Hero is dead!

CLAUDIO Hero, my love!

HERO Claudio, when you said those terrible things to me on our wedding day, I nearly died. But I am alive, and I still love you.

'Hero, my love!'

FATHER FRANCIS   This is a happy day! Come with me to
the church, everyone. It's time for the wedding!

BENEDICK   Wait. There will be two weddings today,
Father Francis, not just one. Where is Beatrice?

BEATRICE   (*Taking off her mask*) I'm here, Benedick.

BENEDICK   Beatrice, will you marry me?

LEONATO   This is wonderful!

DON PEDRO   They're in love! What did I tell you, Claudio?
Our friend Benedick, the married man!

HERO   Well, Beatrice, are you going to answer him?

BEATRICE   Benedick, I'll marry you if it makes you happy.

BENEDICK   No, no, Beatrice, if you marry me, it will make
you happy.

CLAUDIO   Don't start arguing, my friends!

BENEDICK   Claudio is right. Let's not argue – let's kiss.

They kiss, as a messenger enters.

MESSENGER   My lords, the police have found Don John.
They are bringing him back to Messina.

DON PEDRO   We'll think about that tomorrow. Today, we
must think about these weddings.

BENEDICK   Let's have a party first! Musicians – start
playing! Dance, everybody! Enjoy yourselves!

The musicians play, and everyone dances.

EXERCISES

A Checking your understanding

Act 1 *Who said these words in this act?*
1 'Are many of the soldiers hurt?'
2 'It's impossible for anyone to be married and to be happy.'
3 'I hate them all, but I will smile lovingly at them.'
4 'I was hiding. They didn't know that I was listening.'

Act 2 *Write answers to these questions.*
1 When Benedick arrives at the party, what is he wearing?
2 At the party, who asks Hero if she would like to dance?
3 Why is Claudio surprised that Hero wants to marry him?
4 Why does Benedick hide behind the tree in the garden?

Act 3 *In this act, who . . .*
1 tells Beatrice to come into the garden?
2 says that he's got toothache?
3 tells Don Pedro and Claudio to meet him at midnight?
4 shouts 'Hero, my love, give me a kiss!'?

Acts 4 and 5 *Are these sentences true (T) or false (F)?*
1 Hero doesn't agree to marry Claudio.
2 Beatrice asks Benedick to kill Claudio.
3 Borachio thinks that Dogberry is intelligent.
4 Claudio believes that Hero is dead.
5 Benedick is afraid of Claudio.
6 Don John escapes from Messina, but is caught.
7 Claudio marries Hero's cousin.

B Working with language

1 *Use these words to join the sentences together.*

when   but   and then   because

1 Claudio fell in love with Hero. She was so beautiful.
2 Claudio wanted to speak to Hero. He didn't know what to say.
3 Borachio listened secretly to Don Pedro and Claudio. He ran to his master to tell him the news.
4 It was dark. The policemen caught Borachio and Conrade.

2 *Complete these sentences with information from the play.*
1 The night before Hero's wedding, Borachio told Margaret to . . .
2 While Hero and Ursula were talking about Benedick, Beatrice was . . .
3 Don John told Claudio and Don Pedro that Hero . . .
4 If the policemen find people shouting or making too much noise, they must . . .

C Activities

1 The messenger gives Leonato a letter from Don Pedro at the start of the play. You are Don Pedro, writing to your old friend Leonato, with news of the war. Write the letter.
2 You are one of the policemen in Messina. Write a report for your boss, Dogberry, about the night that you and the other policemen caught Don John's wicked men, Borachio and Conrade. Put in as much information as you can.
3 You are Borachio. Write your diary for the night before Hero's wedding. Were you happy to make trouble for

Claudio and Hero, or were you just doing it for the money? What went wrong with your plan? How did you feel when the police caught you?

4 You are Benedick. It is five years after your marriage to Beatrice. Write a letter to Claudio to give him all your news, and ask about him and Hero.

D Project work

1 What other plays do you know by William Shakespeare? Do you know any famous characters from his plays? Write down what you find out.

2 At the end of the play, there are two weddings. Have you ever been to a wedding? In your country, what happens at weddings? Where do people marry? Who comes to the wedding? Is there usually a party after the wedding? Write down as much information as you can.

3 Why is this play called a comedy? Do you think it is funny? If so, why? What other books, stories, plays, films or television programmes make you laugh? Write a list, and try to say why each one is funny.

GLOSSARY

argue to talk or shout angrily when you don't agree with someone

believe to feel sure that something is true or right

brave not afraid of anything

cousin your uncle's or aunt's child

enter to come in

faint to fall down suddenly because you are ill or get bad news

fall in love to find out, suddenly, that you love someone
gentleman a man of good family
good-looking beautiful, handsome
hate opposite of 'to love'
heart (in this play) a person's feelings and hopes
idea a plan that comes into your head suddenly
idiot a stupid person
joke to say (or to do) something funny
kiss to touch someone with the lips in a loving way
lady a title for a woman of good family
lion a large and dangerous wild animal found in Africa (we say
   'as brave as a lion')
lord a title for a man of good family
mask a cover that you put over your face to hide it
messenger someone who brings news or information
musician someone who plays a musical instrument
priest a person who works for the church, a church leader
prince the son of a king or queen
public house a place where people meet, often in the evenings,
   to drink and eat
servant someone who works (for example, cooking or cleaning)
   in another person's house
sir a polite way to speak to a man who is more important than
   you
toothache when one of your teeth hurts
truth something that is true
war fighting between countries or large groups of people
wedding when a man and a woman marry (often in a church)